THE GREAT DEPRESSION

AMERICAN ERAS: DEFINING MOMENTS

MARTIN GITLIN

Published in the United States of America by Cherry Lake Publishing Group
Ann Arbor, Michigan
www.cherrylakepublishing.com

Content Adviser: Kevin Whinnery, MA, History
Reading Adviser: Beth Walker Gambro, MS, Ed., Reading Consultant, Yorkville, IL
Photo Credits: © Photo by Dorthea Lange/Library of Congress/LOC Control No. 2017759225, cover, 1; © Photo by Russell Lee/Library of Congress/LOC Control No. 2017741299, 5; © Everett Collection/Shutterstock, 7, 8, 9, 13, 14, 19, 21, 25, 26, 28; © Photo by Harris & Ewing/Picryl, 10; © Photo by Dorthea Lange/Library of Congress/LOC Control No. 2017769964, 15; © Wikimedia/Photo by NOAA George E. Marsh Album, 16; © stock35/Shutterstock, 20; © Skye Studio LK/Shutterstock, 22

Copyright © 2022 by Cherry Lake Publishing Group
All rights reserved. No part of this book may be reproduced or utilized in any form or by any means without written permission from the publisher.

Cherry Lake Press is an imprint of Cherry Lake Publishing Group.

Library of Congress Cataloging-in-Publication Data
Names: Gitlin, Marty, author.
Title: The Great Depression / by Martin Gitlin.
Description: Ann Arbor, Michigan : Cherry Lake Publishing Group, [2022] | Series: American eras: defining moments | Includes index.
Identifiers: LCCN 2021007857 (print) | LCCN 2021007858 (ebook) | ISBN 9781534187375 (hardcover) | ISBN 9781534188778 (paperback) | ISBN 9781534190177 (pdf) | ISBN 9781534191570 (ebook)
Subjects: LCSH: Depressions–1929–United States–Juvenile literature. | United States–Economic conditions–1918-1945–Juvenile literature.
Classification: LCC HB3717 1929 .G554 2022 (print) | LCC HB3717 1929 (ebook) | DDC 330.973/0916–dc23
LC record available at https://lccn.loc.gov/2021007857
LC ebook record available at https://lccn.loc.gov/2021007858

Cherry Lake Publishing Group would like to acknowledge the work of the Partnership for 21st Century Learning, a Network of Battelle for Kids. Please visit http://www.battelleforkids.org/networks/p21 for more information.

Printed in the United States of America
Corporate Graphics

ABOUT THE AUTHOR

Martin Gitlin has written more than 150 educational books. He also won more than 45 awards during his 11-year career as a newspaper journalist. Gitlin lives in Cleveland, Ohio.

TABLE OF CONTENTS

INTRODUCTION 4

CHAPTER 1
The Great Depression 6

CHAPTER 2
The Pain of No Rain 12

CHAPTER 3
The Impact on Families and Everyday Life 18

CHAPTER 4
A New Deal..24

RESEARCH & ACT 28
TIMELINE 29
FURTHER RESEARCH 30
GLOSSARY 31
INDEX 32

INTRODUCTION

The U.S. economy appeared to be thriving in the 1920s. Most Americans felt confident in the future of their country. They spent more money now than they ever did in the past, often on things they couldn't afford.

People bought items on **credit**. They used **installment** plans. This system allowed them to pay off expensive goods a month at a time with **interest**. It allowed people to have what were considered luxury items. During that time, those things included cars, vacuum cleaners, and radios.

But this system created a problem. Many Americans didn't save money in banks. They went into **debt** because they couldn't pay off what they bought.

"Buy now, pay later" became the philosophy of many middle-class Americans during the Roaring Twenties.

Many Americans also purchased **stocks**. They depended on the businesses they invested in to make profits. But this proved to be a bad gamble. Americans lost millions of dollars when those businesses began to fail.

The stock market crashed in late October 1929. The event ruined many lives. The economy was struggling. The result was the Great Depression of the 1930s.

CHAPTER 1

The Great Depression

Few Americans could have imagined the depth of suffering they would soon feel when entering the new decade. The market crash of 1929 sent the economy reeling. But that wasn't the worst of it.

A total of 650 banks went out of business in 1929, and the total number more than doubled the following year. Many people lost all the money they had saved. Fewer banks meant less money was being borrowed because there was a limited amount of money being supplied. This led to a dramatic decrease in the price of services and goods, also known as a deflation. It also meant that people were no longer able to buy using credit since there were fewer banks able to issue credit. Americans were still reeling from

In 1930, over 20,000 companies filed for bankruptcy.

the debt they took on during the 1920s. They didn't have money to spend. The lack of paying customers meant reduced **income** for many other businesses. They were forced to fire employees or even declare **bankruptcy**. Only 3 percent of American workers were **unemployed** in the late 1920s. But after the market crash, that percentage more than tripled to 16 percent by 1931 and continued to rise.

In 1930, about 12,000 people lost their jobs every single day.

Rallies and marches were organized to protest the declining economy caused by monopolies.

People lost their homes. Many went hungry. They couldn't afford food. Some went as far as rioting and smashing grocery store windows to get food for themselves and their families. People were at their breaking point.

President Hoover created the President's Organization of Unemployment Relief (POUR) to assist with state and private relief agencies, such as The Red Cross, Salvation Army, and the YMCA. (Chairman of The Red Cross pictured with President Hoover.)

The stock market crashed only 8 months after U.S. President Herbert Hoover was elected. For 4 long years, he tried to stop the Great Depression. But he was unsuccessful. Many city dwellers were forced to build and live in shacks. These areas were called "Hoovervilles" in mockery of the poor job the president was doing.

By 1933, an astounding 1 in 4 Americans of working age, or 25 percent, were unemployed. By then, President Hoover had been voted out of office in favor of Franklin D. Roosevelt.

CHAPTER 2

The Pain of No Rain

President Roosevelt faced disaster when he entered the White House in 1933. The average American family income had fallen from $2,300 to $1,500 per year since 1929. Three or even four families began crowding together in one shack to save money. Others lived in caves or even sewer pipes.

Most Americans couldn't afford medical or dental care. Some had little money for food despite low prices. There were multiple reasons for this, and one of those reasons was due to demand. During the 1920s, there was a surplus of food. But when that demand suddenly fell, the prices reflected this—low demand,

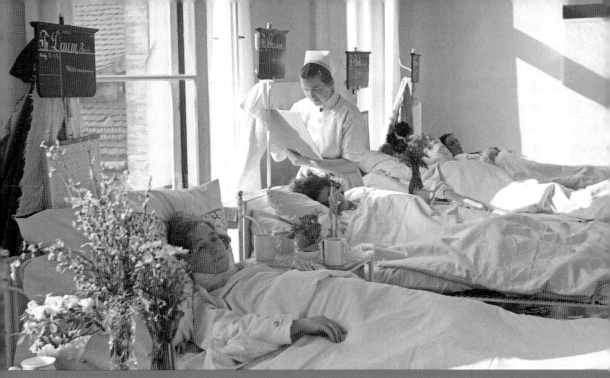

Due to lack of medical care, the main causes of death in the 1930s were heart disease, cancer, pneumonia, infections, and parasitic disorders.

low price. There was food, but since it wasn't being purchased, it was, unfortunately, being destroyed. Many families did without milk or meat. Hunger became common. At least 110 people starved to death in New York City in 1934. Many others suffered health problems from **malnutrition**.

The Dust Bowl gets its name from an AP reporter, Robert Geiger, who used it to describe the aftermath of the Black Sunday dust storm.

But that wasn't all. The worst **drought** in 300 years caused even more great suffering. This event became known as the Dust Bowl. During this time, severe dust storms destroyed the land by blowing away the soil. Crops shriveled and died from poor soil and lack of rain.

Because of the severe dust storms, many families were forced to travel in search of work.

The worst dust storm, Black Sunday, happened on April 14, 1935, in Oklahoma, with over 3 million tons of topsoil blown off the Great Plains.

In 1931, severe storms destroyed most of the crops in plains areas of the Midwest and South. The following year, 14 storms were reported. This number increased to 38 by 1932. Farmers were struggling. They even resorted to killing pigs to reduce their supply and raise prices again. But they were criticized for wasting edible pork.

The devastating dust storms that made it impossible to grow food covered 75 percent of the country by the end of 1934. To make matters worse, a record heat wave worsened in 1936. The heat killed as many as 5,000 Americans that year. According to Weather Underground, a weather service that provides weather-related information, the heat wave of 1936 directly killed 1,693 people. Over 3,000 people drowned as they attempted to cool off in lakes and rivers.

The droughts didn't end until 1941. By that time, the Great Depression was finally over, but not without leaving an unfortunate mark on families.

Woody and the Dust Bowl

Among those affected by the Dust Bowl was folk singer Woody Guthrie. He wrote songs about that event. Guthrie was born and raised in Oklahoma. He later moved to an area of Texas that was severely damaged by the Dust Bowl. Guthrie wrote a song titled "So Long, It's Been Good to Know You" about one dust storm in 1935. He continued to write songs about the Dust Bowl after moving to California to seek work. Guthrie became known as "The Dust Bowl Troubadour." Should songwriters today write more songs that spotlight the world's problems? Why or why not?

CHAPTER 3

The Impact on Families and Everyday Life

The Great Depression made a huge impact on American families. Many people married later in life than in the past. This resulted in fewer babies being born for a long period of time. Fewer people were getting divorced, but not out of choice. Couples couldn't afford the legal fees and or separate housing. The Depression forced them to stay together. In fact, it even forced some families to live together in cramped apartments or single-family homes.

Losing health benefits was one of the risks that came with getting a divorce.

In December 1933, a record-breaking number of 140,000 children were in orphanages.

While the Great Depression forced some families together, other families were torn apart. By the end of the 1930s, 1.5 million women were living apart from their husbands. More than 200,000 children had become homeless. Their parents were unable to care for them. These children either entered orphanages or traveled by train looking for work.

"Hooverville" huts were created out of cardboard, tin, lumber, glass, and tar paper.

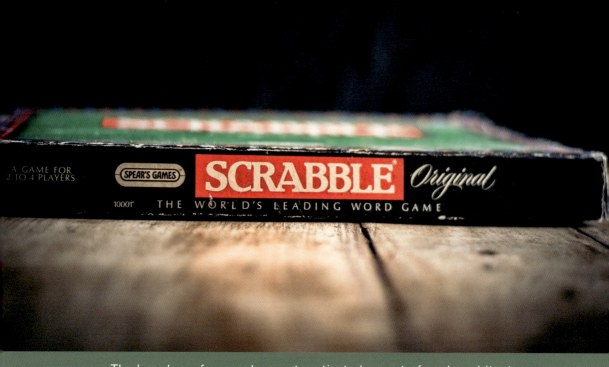

The boredom of unemployment motivated an out-of-work architect, Alfred Mosher Butts, to create Scrabble in 1933.

Those who managed to suffer through the hard times lived by former President Calvin Coolidge's quote, "Eat it up, wear it out, make it do, or do without." Coolidge was the president during most of the 1920s. The Great Depression forced families to live within their means. Their lives were a stark contrast from the 1920s. Instead of shopping at the grocery store, families planted gardens and grew their own food. Some cities even converted empty lots to gardens. These were nicknamed "thrift gardens." Clothes were patched and handed down instead of being replaced by new ones. **Potlucks** became an inexpensive way to socialize.

The Great Depression forced families to get creative. Instead of going to the movies, which were popular just a decade before, people stayed home. They played card and board games. Neighbors would get together for game night. It was during the 1930s that Scrabble and Monopoly were invented and became popular.

Many people during this time already owned radios, which also provided entertainment. Radio soap operas and comedy programs became a popular alternative to the movies for a time. Despite being unable to afford tickets to sporting events, families could follow the games by listening to sportscasters on the radio.

They Said What?

Journalist Tom Brokaw said the following about American togetherness during the Great Depression: *"The greatest generation was formed first by the Great Depression. They shared everything—meals, jobs, clothing."* Do you feel your generation has the same desire to help other Americans? What can you do to aid the lives of those who are struggling?

CHAPTER 4

A New Deal

The top goal for President Roosevelt was putting people back to work. Unemployment had soared to 25 percent when he began his first term.

The problem was that businesses were failing all over the country. Few jobs were available. So, Roosevelt decided to create them. This meant the government had to spend billions of dollars creating and paying for new job programs. These were later called the "New Deal."

The New Deal increased government debt from $22 billion to $43 billion. But it did create jobs. The New Deal put people to work.

The Civilian Conservation Corps (CCC) gave about 2,750,000 young men jobs doing numerous conservation projects such as irrigation, pest control, and tree planting.

They paved roads and constructed buildings. The Tennessee Valley Authority project provided work building dams. Many other projects were established to employ people, including writers, artists, and photographers.

The New Deal also served to help farmers. Farmers were paid to cut **production** because people were buying less food. Farmers were also paid to learn more effective planting and soil conservation methods. The new roads and bridges being built helped farmers move their crops to market more easily.

The National Youth Administration (NYA) made it feasible for 1.5 million high school students and 600,000 college students to continue their education by providing part-time jobs.

The New Deal also aided the banking system. It ensured that banks couldn't go out of business without giving people the money they had **deposited**.

Roosevelt worked to explain his New Deal to the people. He wanted Americans to believe in the programs and feel confident about their country again. He began a series of radio speeches he called "Fireside Chats" to explain his ideas.

Another round of the New Deal authorized $4 billion in programs in 1935. It provided part-time work for college students. And the Works Progress Administration gave an estimated 3.5 million Americans jobs constructing more roads, buildings, and bridges.

The New Deal finally helped lift the United States out of the Great Depression in 1939. Soon, the country put millions to work creating materials for World War II. The United States would emerge from that conflict with the strongest economy in the world.

The CCC and Native Americans

Among the many New Deal programs launched by President Roosevelt was the Civilian Conservation Corps. It put 3 million young men to work building and restoring U.S. natural resources. And an offshoot of that project benefited Native Americans. The Indian Emergency Conservation Work created many jobs. It employed about 85,000 Native Americans preserving tribal land and promoting ranching and farming. Has the plight of Native Americans been addressed enough in the modern era?

By 1939, the national income was back to the level of 1929.

Research & Act

The end of the Great Depression wasn't the end of poverty in the United States. The poverty rate remains high today. Research where the poverty level in your area is the highest and take steps to help. Ask family members to help or organize a food drive at your school. You can take food to a food bank or to senior centers. Or you can help serve meals at shelters. You can give your used toys to children in need. And used clothes are always wanted at thrift and secondhand shops. It's also important to raise the awareness of your friends about poverty in your town so they can help too.

Timeline

- **Summer 1930:** The Dust Bowl begins with drought conditions in the eastern half of the United States.

- **February 1931:** Food riots break out in parts of the United States.

- **1932:** The U.S. unemployment rate reaches nearly 24 percent.

- **November 8, 1932:** Franklin Roosevelt is elected president.

- **1933:** New Deal programs are launched.

- **May 18, 1933:** The Tennessee Valley Authority is created to put people to work building dams.

- **June 16, 1933:** The Public Works Administration is established.

- **1935:** The Second New Deal begins.

- **April 14, 1935:** A huge dust storm hits the Midwest. The event is called Black Sunday.

- **1936:** Unemployment falls to 17 percent.

- **1939:** The Great Depression ends.

Further Research

BOOKS

Lassieur, Allison. *The Dust Bowl: An Interactive History Adventure.* North Mankato, MN: Capstone Press, 2009.

Mullenbach, Cheryl. *The Great Depression for Kids: Hardship and Hope in 1930s America with 21 Activities.* Chicago, IL: Chicago Review Press, 2015.

WEBSITES

Ducksters—U.S. History: The Great Depression
https://www.ducksters.com/history/us_1900s/great_depression.php

Britannica Kids: New Deal
https://kids.britannica.com/kids/article/New-Deal/390817

Glossary

bankruptcy (BANK-rupt-see) a legal agreement created when people owe more money than they have, allowing them to settle their debts with their creditors

credit (KREH-dit) to buy now and pay later

debt (DET) money owed to another person or company

deposited (dih-PAH-zuh-tuhd) to add to something, such as a bank account

drought (DROUT) long dry spell caused by lack of rain

income (IN-kuhm) amount of money earned

installment (in-STAHL-muhnt) monthly or yearly payment to pay off a purchase made on credit

interest (IN-trist) the money paid by a borrower for the use of borrowed money

malnutrition (mal-noo-TRISH-uhn) harmful condition caused by lack of nutritious food

potlucks (paht-LUHKZ) meals where each guest brings food to share

production (pruh-DUHK-shuhn) act of growing or making something

stocks (STAHKS) certificates that represent part ownership of a business or corporation

unemployed (uhn-ihm-PLOYD) the state of being out of work

INDEX

babies, 18
bankruptcy, 7
banks/banking, 4, 6, 26
Black Sunday dust storm, 14, 16, 29
bridges, 25, 27
building construction, 25, 27

children, 20
Civilian Conservation Corps (CCC), 25, 27
clothes, 22
college students, 26, 27
conservation projects, 25
Coolidge, Calvin, 22
credit, 4, 5, 6

dams, 25, 29
deaths, 13, 17
debt
    government, 24
    personal, 4, 7
deflation, 6
divorce, 18, 19
drought, 12-17, 29
Dust Bowl, 14-17, 29
dust storms, 14, 15, 16-17, 29

economy, U.S., 4, 6, 9, 27
education, 26
entertainment, 22-23

families, 18-23
farmers, 25
Fireside Chats, 26
food, 12-13, 16-17, 22, 25, 29

games, 23
gardens, 22
Geiger, Robert, 14
Great Depression, 6-11
    end of, 27, 29
    entertainment during, 22-23
    impact on families and everyday life, 18-23
    introduction, 4-5
    timeline, 29
Great Plains, 16
Guthrie, Woody, 17

health problems, 12, 13, 19
heat wave, 17
high school students, 26
homelessness, 11, 12, 20
Hoover, Herbert, 10, 11
Hoovervilles, 11, 21
hunger, 13

income, 7
    average, 12
    national, 28
Indian Emergency Conservation Work, 27
installment plans, 4
interest, 4
investments, 5

jobs, 7, 8, 11, 20, 29.
    See also unemployment
    and the New Deal, 24-27

luxury items, 4

malnutrition, 13
market crash. See stock market crash
marriage, 18
middle class, 5
monopolies, 9
Monopoly (game), 23
movies, 23

National Youth Administration (NYA), 26
Native Americans, 27
natural resources, 27
New Deal, 24-27, 29

orphans/orphanages, 20

potlucks, 22
POUR (President's Organization of Unemployment Relief), 10
poverty, 28
prices, 12-13, 16
protests, 9
Public Works Administration, 29

radios, 4, 23
rain, lack of, 12-17
Red Cross, The, 10
relief agencies, 10
road construction, 25, 27
Roaring Twenties, 5
Roosevelt, Franklin D., 11, 12, 24, 26, 27, 29

Salvation Army, 10
savings, 4, 6
Scrabble, 22, 23
starvation, 13
stock market crash, 5, 6, 11

Tennessee Valley Authority (TVA), 25, 29
thrift gardens, 22
timeline, 29

unemployment, 7, 8, 11, 22, 24, 29. See also jobs

work. See jobs
Works Progress Administration, 27
World War II, 27

YMCA, 10